5G: Still Life

Learn about realism.

Graeme Smith

PUBLISHED ON AMAZON.com
by
LABYRINTH BOOKS

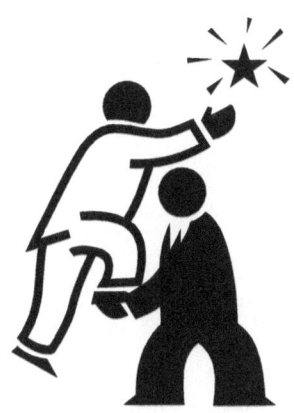

DEDICATION:

This book is dedicated to my family.
Hele-ly (Ly).
> my wife:

Ingrid.
> our daughter:

Marie.
> my former wife:

Fiona, Natalie and Michael
> our children:

Georgie
> Michael's wife:

Pearl, Kiki and Martha.
> their children:

They have put up with me for many years and I thank them for that.
I hope this book gives an insight into what occupied me much of the time.
All have done worthwhile and interesting things in the absence of my help.
I congratulate them for their achievements.

SUPPORT:

Support the International Artist magazine
– contact: editor@internationalartist.com

Support the Australian Artist magazine

– **contact:** editor@australianartist.com

HOW TO USE THIS BOOK.

Usually people don't think through things to the level they need to.
Because of that, they have projects instead of tasks on their "to do" list.
That leads to procrastination because it hasn't been broken down to a task level.
So go through your book once to understand it then go through it again.

Start at the PART of the book that you think you should start at.
Make notes of the steps you will need to take and the resources required.
Use the notes to make a step by step system to implement the particular ideas.
You don't have to refer back to the original, if you've created **YOUR** system.

The first question you have to ask and answer is "Why is this being done?"
How does this align with where you want to get to?
What are the strategic implications of doing this?
Does this fit in with getting to your goal in the shortest and fastest amount of time?
What would it be like if it were totally successful?
Define it - what is success for this project and how will you know?

Now brainstorm all the tasks are involved.
It's important not to go linear too fast, step 1, step 2, step 3, and step 4.
You end up cutting off options.
As you plan step 1, 2, and 3, there is a specific step that might be number 4.
If you start steps too quickly, other ways of doing 1, 2 and 3 may not appear.

The first 1/3 of a brainstorming session is easy - just generate lots of ideas.
The second third is a little bit more challenging.
Go through those ideas and see where they lead to.
Then push yourself to think outside the box for that's often where the big idea is!
That's where the most powerful way of getting the project done the fastest – is.

Most never get to that level and so end up short-changing themselves.
Then their project takes longer and they also set themselves up to procrastinate.
This final brainstorming part of the equation is incredibly important.

Once you fully brainstorm a project put your options into a linear sequence.
Then you can figure out what you've overlooked and everything becomes obvious.
Get your tasks in order, add missing steps, lay out your task list for the project.

Organize tasks into a linear process and decide what things can you start immediately?

Step one is to start with no dependency on things that have to occur before them. There might be step 5 or 6 or 20 that don't rely on anything else to get done. You can get started on them right away!

Write what you think of at the time and also cross off things as you do them. Add in stuff that is relevant from time to time.

As a basis for learning about realism use photographs.

Focus on learning what you can.
Action with materials = technique.
Practiced techniques = skill.
Habitual technique + skill = style.

Continue with the subject matter you want to paint really well.
That way you are continuing down the correct path (for you).
Your focus is always on portraits, landscapes, the sea, or whatever you like.

Don't just select animals focus on one (tiger, cat, horse).
Then even from the start you can become a specialist.
Also focus on something you are interested in.
This will help maintain the necessary motivation while you learn.

Understand your animal, house, landscape, or whatever you choose.
Over time you will develop the individual paining skills needed.
You will also know how to paint your subject your way.

Eventually you can focus on another subject.
If it is related to your original theme you will learn much quicker.
From one breed of dog to another is an example.
Then from one kind of animal to another.

You'll note the similarities and also the differences.
You could even progress from portraits to head and shoulders studies.
Later these might be full figures.

Follow this pattern for long enough, and you'll be able to paint anything!
People who do things well also do them faster than those who don't.
That applies to painting just as much as anything else.
It's one of the indicators of skill.

By now you should notice that repetition helps skill development.
Several small paintings are better for learning.
Larger ones take more time and that's how you apply what you have learnt.

Skill in art, sport or even medicine is basically the same phenomenon.
It's practiced behaviour in action.
Most artists don't do anywhere near enough to develop any real skill.

INDEX: STILL LIFE.

Still Life   12
Real Still Life.   14
Observed Still Life 1.   34
Observed Still Life 2.   58
Imaginary Still Life.   80

WHERE NEXT?   **115**
NOT NOW: **117**
SEND TO: **118**

STILL LIFE

Photographs are a basis for learning about realism.
Any photograph is of something.
Continue with the subject matter you want to paint really well.
Then you are continuing down the correct path (for you).
Your focus is always on portraits, landscapes, the sea, or whatever you fancy.

Select any still life but focus on just one (stem in a vase).
Then even from the start you can become a specialist.
You will also focus on something you are interested in.
This will help maintain the necessary motivation while you learn.

You get to understand your still life subjects.
Over time you will develop the individual paining skills needed.
You will also know how to paint your subject your way.

Eventually you can focus on another subject.
You'll note the similarities and also the differences.
Because they are related to your original theme you will learn much quicker.
From one type of still life to another is an example.
Then from still life to other flowers could be a pathway.
Follow this pattern for long enough, and you'll be able to paint anything!
People who do things well also do them faster than those who don't.
That applies to painting just as much as anything else.
It's one of the indicators of skill.

You should notice that repetition helps your own skill development.
Skill in art, sport or even medicine is basically the same phenomenon.
It's practiced behaviour in action.
Most artists don't do anywhere near enough to develop real skill.

A number of experiments at the same time increases productivity.
For you reduce wasted time.

If you run into a dead-end with one painting move to another for a fresh start. **When the initial painting is returned to, there will be a different attitude.** Otherwise set it aside again.

Usually you'll find most works will finish fresh and roughly about the same time.

Working on a number of paintings at the same time also saves materials.

A particular colour can be applied to the experiment for which it was intended.

BUT there are bound to be others where that same colour will be appropriate.

When you buy paint, buy in quantity, but only use as needed.

Avoid major works.

They take time (years), usually done slowly and are often large and complex.

You'll tend to labour over them as you try to do your best.

Instead occasionally do a slightly larger experiment.

Focus on learning what you can.

Action with materials = technique.

Practiced techniques = skill.

Habitual technique + skill = style.

REAL STILL LIFE.

FIRST Experience Unit:

UNIT 1: Experiment 1

Copy or photocopy or print out a black and white MMM image you have chosen.

Materials:

Your choice of non-paint, opaque or transparent paint (black and white).

Brush (if using paint).

Begin:

Paint the MMM image in black and white.

Match the original tones.

Notice the shape of the still life.

Conclude:

Clean up.

UNIT 1: Experiment 2

Copy or photocopy or print out a black and white MMM image you have chosen.

Materials:

Your choice of non-paint, opaque or transparent paint.

Brush (if using paint), white paper (small).

Begin:

Copy the still life from your MMM image.

Preliminary drawing in thin paint.

Establish overall shape of the still life.

Keep the painting broad.

Then:

Use a bigger brush with black and white

Notice the shape of the still life.

Conclude:

Clean up.

UNIT 1: Experiment 3

Copy or photocopy or print out a black and white MMM image you have chosen.

Materials:

Your choice of non-paint, opaque or transparent paint (black and white).

Large brush (if using paint), white paper (small).

Begin:

Copy the still life from your MMM image.

Preliminary drawing in thin paint.

Establish overall shape of the still life.

Keep the painting broad.

Then:

Use a bigger brush with black and white

Change from the original tones.

Notice the shape of the still life.

Conclude:

Clean up.

UNIT 1: Experiment 4

Copy or photocopy or print out a coloured MMM image you have chosen.

Materials:

Your choice of non-paint, opaque or transparent paint (black and white).

Large brush (if using paint), white paper (small).

Begin:

Copy the still life from your MMM image.

Preliminary drawing in thin paint with brush.

Block in darkest and lightest areas with thin paint.

Establish overall shape of the still life keeping the painting simple and broad.

Check the relationships between the different parts relative to each other.

Then:

Use a bigger brush with black and white

Copy the original tones.

Conclude:

Clean up.

UNIT 1: Experiment 5

Copy or photocopy or print out a coloured MMM image you have chosen.

Materials:

Your choice of non-paint, opaque or transparent paint (dark and light).

Large brush (if using paint), white paper (small).

Begin:

Copy the still life from your MMM image.

Preliminary drawing in thin paint with brush.

Block in darkest and lightest areas with thin paint.

Establish overall shape of the still life.

Keep the painting simple and broad.

Check the relationships between the different parts relative to each other.

Then:

Use a bigger brush with dark and light paint

Copy the original tones.

Conclude:

Clean up.

UNIT 1: Experiment 6

Copy or photocopy or print out a coloured MMM image you have chosen.

Materials:

Your choice of non-paint, opaque or transparent paint (dark and light).

Large brush (if using paint), toned or coloured paper (small).

Begin:

Copy the still life from your MMM image.

Preliminary drawing in thin paint with brush.

Block in darkest and lightest areas with thin paint.

Establish overall shape of the still life keeping the painting simple and broad.

Check the relationships between the different parts relative to each other.

Then:

Use a bigger brush with dark and light paint

Copy the original tones.

Conclude:

Clean up.

Further thoughts:

Copy other images of still life subjects.

Use dark and light paint (or non-paint).

Establish overall shape of the still life.

Keep the painting simple and broad.

Check the relationships between the different parts relative to each other.

Note the spaces in between these areas.

SECOND Experience Unit:

UNIT 2: Experiment 1

Modify, copy, photocopy or print a specific coloured MMM image you have chosen.

Materials:

Your choice of non-paint, opaque or transparent paint (dark and light).

Large brush (if using paint), toned or coloured paper (small).

Begin:

Copy the still life from your MMM image.

Preliminary drawing in thin paint with brush.

Block in darkest and lightest areas with thin paint.

Establish overall shape of the still life.

Keep the painting simple and broad.

Check the relationships between the different parts relative to each other.

Then:

Use a bigger brush with dark and light paint

Copy the original tones.

Conclude:

Clean up.

UNIT 2: Experiment 2

A specific coloured MMM image if possible taken by you.

Materials:

Choose non-paint, opaque or transparent paint (dark and light + a local colour).

Local colour is the approximate colour of things (black cat, brown dog).

Large brush (if using paint), white paper (small).

Begin:

Copy still life from your MMM image.

Preliminary drawing in thin paint with brush.

Block in darkest and lightest areas with thin paint.

Establish overall shape of the still life.

Keep the painting simple and broad.

Check the relationships between the different parts relative to each other.

Then:

Use a bigger brush with dark and light paint to show the original tones.

Use more dark and light paint to show form and shape.

Use the other colour to add local (as in the still life) colour.

This only needs to approximate the still life colour.

Do NOT overwork the experiment.

Many details you know are there may not be shown.

Conclude:

Clean up.

UNIT 2: Experiment 3

Coloured MMM image used in the previous experiment.

Materials:

Choose non-paint, opaque or transparent paint (dark and light + a local colour).

Large brush (if using paint), white paper (small).

Begin:

Copy still life from your MMM image.

Preliminary drawing in thin paint with brush.

Block in darkest and lightest areas with thin paint.

Establish overall shape of the still life.

Keep the painting simple and broad.

Check the relationships between the different parts relative to each other.

Note the spaces in between.

Then:

Use dark and light paint to show the original tones.

Use more dark and light paint to show form and shape.

Add local (as in the still life) colour.

This only needs to approximate the still life colour.

Do NOT overwork the experiment.

Many details you know are there may not be shown.

Conclude:

Clean up.

UNIT 2: Experiment 4

Coloured MMM image used in the previous experiment.

Materials:

Choose non-paint, opaque or transparent paint (dark and light + a local colour).

Large brush (if using paint), white toned or coloured paper (small).

Begin:

Copy still life from your MMM image.

Preliminary drawing in thin paint with brush.

Block in darkest and lightest areas with thin paint.

Establish overall shape of the still life keeping the painting simple and broad.

Check the relationships between the different parts relative to each other.

Note the spaces in between.

Then:

Use dark and light paint to show the original tones.

Use more dark and light paint to show form and shape.

Add local (as in the still life) colour although this only needs to approximate the still life colour.

Develop your experiment but do NOT overwork it.

Gradually modify the tones and colours.

Many details may not be shown.

Conclude:

Clean up.

UNIT 2: Experiment 5

Coloured MMM image used in the previous experiment.

Materials:

Choose non-paint, opaque or transparent paint (dark and light + a warm and cool colour).

Two brushes (if using paint), white toned or coloured paper (a little larger).

Begin:

Copy still life from your MMM image.

Preliminary drawing in thin paint with brush.

Block in darkest and lightest areas with thin paint.

Establish overall shape of the still life.

Keep the painting simple and broad.

Check the relationships between the different parts relative to each other.

Note the spaces in between.

Then:

Use dark and light paint to show the original tones.

Use more dark and light paint to show form and shape.

Add local (as in the still life) colour.

This only needs to approximate the still life colour.

Develop your experiment but do NOT overwork it.

Gradually modify the tones and colours.

Use warm and cool colours to show depth.

Many details may not be shown.

Conclude:

Clean up.

UNIT 2: Experiment 6

Coloured MMM image used in the previous experiment.

Materials:

Choose non-paint, opaque or transparent paint (dark and light + a warm and cool colour).

Two brushes (if using paint), white toned or coloured paper (a little larger).

Begin:

Copy still life from your MMM image.

Preliminary drawing with brush - block in darkest and lightest areas with thin paint.

Establish overall shape of the still life to keep the experiment simple and broad.

Check the relationships between the different parts relative to each other.

Note the spaces in between.

Then:

Use dark and light paint to show the original tones.

Use more dark and light paint to show form and shape.

Add local (as in the still life) colour.

This only needs to approximate the still life colour.

Develop your experiment but do NOT overwork it.

Gradually modify the tones and colours.

Use warm and cool colours to show depth.

Many details may not be shown.

Conclude:

Clean up.

Further thoughts:

Use other photographs you have taken to explore other views.

Explore different still life arrangements.

THIRD Experience Unit:

UNIT 3: Experiment 1
Modify, copy, photocopy or print out a specific coloured MMM image from memory.
Materials:
Your choice of non-paint, opaque or transparent paint (dark and light also is warm and cool).
A brush (if using paint), white toned or coloured paper (a little larger).
Begin:
Copy still life from your MMM image in dark and light areas with thin paint.
Match original tones.
Use the dark and light colours to show still life form.
Use warm and cool colour to show depth.
Check the relationships between the different parts relative to each other.
Note the spaces in between.
Then:
Add local (as in the still life) colour.
This only needs to approximate the still life colour.
Develop your experiment but do NOT overwork it.
Gradually modify the tones and colours.
Conclude:
Clean up.

UNIT 3: Experiment 2

Memory of a specific coloured MMM image if possible taken by yourself.

Materials:

Your choice of non-paint, opaque or transparent paint (dark, light also warm / cool + local colour).

Two brushes (if using paint), white toned or coloured paper (a little larger).

A piece of glass.

Begin:

Trace still life image onto glass.

Copy still life from your glass tracing in dark and light areas with thin paint.

Match original tones.

Use the dark and light colours to show still life form.

Use warm and cool colour to show depth.

Check the relationships between the different parts relative to each other.

Note the spaces in between.

Then:

Add local (as in the still life) colour.

This only needs to approximate the still life colour.

Develop your experiment but do NOT overwork it.

Gradually modify the tones and colours.

Conclude:

Clean up.

UNIT 3: Experiment 3

Memory of a specific coloured MMM image used in the previous experiment.

Materials:

Your choice of non-paint, opaque or transparent paint (dark, light also warm / cool + local colour).

Two brushes (if using paint), white toned or coloured paper (a little larger).

A tracing glass.

Begin:

Trace still life image onto glass.

Copy still life from your glass tracing in dark and light areas with thin paint.

Match original tones.

Check the relationships between the different parts relative to each other.

Note the spaces in between.

Then:

Use the dark and light colours but vary from the original tones.

Use the dark and light colours to show still life form.

Add local (as in the still life) colour.

This only needs to approximate the still life colour.

Develop your experiment but do NOT overwork it.

Gradually modify the tones and colours.

Use warm and cool colour to show depth.

Conclude:

Clean up.

UNIT 3: Experiment 4

Memory of a specific coloured MMM image used in the previous experiment.

Materials:

Your choice of non-paint, opaque or transparent paint (dark, light also warm / cool + local colour).

Two brushes (if using paint), white toned or coloured paper (a little larger).

A tracing glass.

Begin:

Trace still life image onto glass.

Copy still life from your glass tracing in dark and light areas with thin paint.

Match original tones.

Check the relationships between the different parts relative to each other.

Note the spaces in between.

Then:

Use the dark and light colours but vary from the original tones.

Use the dark and light colours to show still life form.

Add local (as in the still life) colour which only needs to approximate the still life colour.

Develop your experiment but do NOT overwork it.

Gradually modify the tones and colours and using warm and cool colour to show depth.

Do not attempt too much detail - only paint what can be seen by a viewer.

Conclude:

Clean up.

UNIT 3: Experiment 5

Memory of a specific coloured MMM image used in the previous experiment.

Materials:

Your choice of non-paint, opaque or transparent paint (dark, light also warm / cool + local colour).

Two brushes (if using paint), white toned or coloured paper (a little larger).

A tracing glass.

Begin:

Trace still life image onto glass.

Copy still life from your glass tracing in dark and light areas with thin paint - match original tones.

Check the relationships between different parts relative to each other - note the spaces between.

Then:

Use the dark and light colours but vary from the original tones - to show still life form.

Add local (as in the still life) colour which only needs to approximate the still life colour.

Develop your experiment but do NOT overwork it.

Gradually modify the tones and colours.

Use soft and hard edges for modelling.

Boundaries between shapes should not always be too sharp or clear cut.

A soft irregular transition is required from time to time.

Gradually modify tones and colours – for example use warm and cool colour to show depth.

Suggest texture by dry-brush or sgraffito techniques - thicker paint may be required.

Do not attempt too much detail - only paint what can be seen by a viewer.

Conclude:

Clean up.

UNIT3: Experiment 6

Memory of a specific coloured MMM image used in the previous experiment.

Materials:

Your choice of non-paint, opaque or transparent paint (dark, light also warm / cool + local colour).

Two brushes (if using paint), white toned or coloured paper (a little larger).

A tracing glass.

Begin:

Trace still life image onto glass.

Copy still life from your glass tracing in dark and light areas with thin paint - match original tones.

Check the relationships between different parts relative to each other - note the spaces between.

Then:

Use the dark and light colours but vary from the original tones - to show still life form.

Add local (as in the still life) colour which only needs to approximate the still life colour.

Develop your experiment but do NOT overwork it.

Gradually modify the tones and colours.

Use soft and hard edges for modelling.

Boundaries between shapes should not always be too sharp or clear cut.

A soft irregular transition is required from time to time.

Gradually modify tones and colours – for example use warm and cool colour to show depth.

Suggest texture by dry-brush or sgraffito techniques - thicker paint may be required.

Do not attempt too much detail - only paint what can be seen by a viewer.

Conclude:

Clean up.

Further thoughts:

Use memories of other photographs you have taken to explore other views.

DEVELOPMENT: Extensions

In the Development extension activities:

Draw on what you have learnt.

You can link what you have learned to your own goals.

DEVELOPMENT: Extension 1

Copy or photocopy or print out the MMM image you have chosen.

Materials:

Use the SAME materials as used in a previous experiment from Unit One.

Use the SAME MMM image as used in a previous experiment Unit One.

Begin:

BUT repeat only one of the experiments.

DEVELOPMENT: Extension 2

Modify copy or photocopy or print out of the MMM image you have chosen.

Materials:

Use the SAME materials as used in a previous experiment from Unit Two.

Use the SAME MMM image as used in a previous experiment Unit Two.

Begin:

BUT repeat only one of the experiments.

DEVELOPMENT: Extension 3

Modify copy or photocopy or print of the MMM image you have chosen from memory.

Materials:

Use the SAME materials as used in a previous experiment from Unit Three.

Use the SAME MMM image as used in a previous experiment Unit Three.

Begin:

BUT repeat only one of the experiments.

CONGRATULATIONS.

You have taken the REALISM pathway.
This continues from the previous pattern of experiments.
The focus is on photographs and pictures as a basis for a continuing search for reality.

This could be the final step to being the artist you want to be.

But perhaps you want to try them all?
Then follow the sequence of MMM experiments as outlined.
There is a logical progression.

The second pathway is based on OBSERVATION.
This focus is a more traditional approach.
But the foundation has been laid with the MMM experiments.

But if your MMM focus is NOT observable this pathway is not for you.
Then you can go straight to the third pathway.

The third pathway is linked to your IMAGINATION.
This focus is more personal.
But again there is a foundation from the MMM experiments.

Your MMM experiments are like the athletes training program.
But the training never stops.
Like an Olympic athlete you want to remain at a high level so keep training.
Your MMM experiments become a normal routine.

Make notes, do sketches and record what you can see.

This is material you can draw on when continuing your MMM experiments. Make a habit to carry a small sketchpad or scraps of paper and a pen or pencil.

Perhaps start each day with a short period of experiments.
Then move to your main artistic tasks.

You'll need to construct YOUR OWN MMM experimental programs.
By now this should not be difficult.

Planning major works could follow from that.
But do them as extensions of your MMM experiments.
A slightly larger experiment can develop into a major work.
Then much of the planning and preparatory work has been done.

STILL LIFE OBSERVED.

Continue with the subject matter you want to paint really well.
Your focus is always on still life or whatever you fancy.

Like the Californian artist don't just select any still life but focus on one.
Then even from the start you can become a specialist.
You will also focus on something you are interested in.
This will help maintain the necessary motivation while you learn.

But now observe your chosen painting focus.
This means you are limited to things you can actually look at.
This is not a problem with a still life focus.

You get to understand still life.
Over time you will develop the individual paining skills needed.
You will also know how to paint your subject your way.

Collect objects that are suitable for using in still life arrangements.
Objects with interesting colours or reflecting surfaces are always handy.
Various interesting forms (shapes) could also be collected.
They're foils in the arrangement so don't have to be complex.
Simple forms like a matchbox, a ball or bottle will find a great deal of use.
Junk shops provide a source for your still life objects.

Move from a general focus to a narrower one.
Instead of an arrangement of things focus on colour schemes.
You'll note the similarities and also the differences.
Because they are all still life you will learn much quicker.

You could progress from one object to several to complex arrangements.
Follow this pattern for long enough, and you'll be able to paint anything!

Make notes, do sketches and record what you can see.
This is material you can draw on when continuing your MMM experiments.
Make a habit to carry a small sketchpad or scraps of paper and a pen or pencil.

Set up MMM experiments right where your observation focus is.
A still life arrangement is an easy fit for this approach.

Your observation helps you understand your objects or plants.
Over time you will develop the individual paining skills needed.
You will also know how to paint your subject your way.

Eventually you can focus on another subject.
If it is related to your original theme you will learn much quicker.
From one set of objects to others but with elements repeated is an example.
Then from one kind of arrangement to another.

People who do things well also do them faster than those who don't.
That applies to painting just as much as anything else.
It's one of the indicators of skill.

Notice that repetition helps your own skill development.
Skill in art, sport or even medicine is basically the same phenomenon.
It's practiced behaviour in action.
Most artists don't do anywhere near enough to develop real skill.

A number of experiments at the same time increases productivity.
If you run into a dead-end with one painting move to another for a fresh start.
When the initial painting is returned to, there will be a different attitude.
Otherwise set it aside again but you reduce wasted time.
Usually you'll find most works will finish fresh and roughly about the same time.

Working on a number of paintings at the same time also saves materials.

A particular colour can be applied to the experiment for which it was intended.

BUT there are bound to be others where that same colour will be appropriate.

When you buy paint, buy in quantity, but only use as needed.

Avoid major works.

They take time (years), usually done slowly and are often large and complex.

You'll tend to labour over them as you try to do your best.

Instead occasionally do a slightly larger experiment.

Focus on learning what you can.

Action with materials = technique.

Practiced techniques = skill.

Habitual technique + skill = style.

Do you have a sketchbook?

You are probably familiar with a sketchbook.

It can be an old book, just as long as you write, scribble, draw, or make notes.

It doesn't really matter whether it has lines or the pages are blank.

It'll end up full of your ideas, or memory aids for your ideas.

Naturally ideas for paintings will be there.

Writing them down is a powerful way to commit thoughts to your memory bank.

Then they are accessible later.

Looking at pages in your sketchbook a later date will refresh those ideas.

That will go beyond what is merely recorded in your book.

Write your ideas and build a bridge from what you see and actions you take.

Do you plan effectively?

Your Ideas sketchbook can be where you start your planning.
Sometimes this will be repetitive, as minor variations are tested.
But they have to be worked through to find out what happens.
Effective planning is the beginnings of effective actions.
Your plans are the test runs for the real world.
Plans don't make anything happen, but they certainly ease the way.
Your preparation can be quite systematic!

How will you get the most from your sketchbook?
You'll always get more from what you draw or write rather than read or hear.
Carry out sensible ideas there's a chance you'll improve on your past efforts.
If you do not try anything then there is no chance of an improvement at all.

This is particularly useful when you are observing fleeting moments.
Sometimes they'll turn out great, but at other times not so.
But you don't need to be brave for there is no risk.

Do enough fleeting experiments and they WILL get better!
You will be able to capture in paint passing moments of life.
They'll have spontaneity that is often lacking in a photographic based artwork.

NOW START: STILL LIFE OBSERVED 1

FIRST Experience Unit:

UNIT 1: Experiment 1

Start with an MMM still life observation.

Materials:

Your choice of (dark, light also warm / cool) non-paint, opaque or transparent paint.

Two brushes (if using paint), white toned or coloured paper (a little larger).

Begin:

Copy still life from your MMM observation.

Use thin paint (large brush).

Only show what is necessary.

Then:

Use the dark and light colours to show still life forms and soft and hard edges for modelling.

Use thin paint before using thick paint and paint smaller parts later.

Boundaries between shapes should not always be too sharp or clear cut.

A soft irregular transition is required from time to time.

Develop your experiment but do NOT overwork it.

Gradually modify tones and colours – for example use warm and cool colour to show depth.

Suggest texture by dry-brush or sgraffito techniques which may require thicker paint.

Do not attempt too much detail - only paint what can be seen by a viewer.

Conclude:

Clean up.

UNIT 1: Experiment 2

Start with the same MMM still life observation as in the previous experiment.

Materials:

Your choice of (dark, light - warm / cool + another colour) non-paint, opaque or transparent paint.

Two brushes (if using paint), white toned or coloured paper (a little larger).

Begin:

Copy one part of the still life from your MMM observation (object).

Use thin paint (large brush).

Only show what is necessary.

Then:

Use the dark and light colours to show still life forms and soft and hard edges for modelling.

Use thin paint before using thick paint and paint smaller parts later.

Boundaries between shapes should not always be too sharp or clear cut.

A soft irregular transition is required from time to time.

Develop your experiment but do NOT overwork it.

Gradually modify tones and colours – for example use warm and cool colour to show depth.

Suggest texture by dry-brush or sgraffito techniques which may require thicker paint.

Do not attempt too much detail - only paint what can be seen by a viewer.

Conclude:

Clean up.

UNIT 1: Experiment 3

Start with the same MMM still life observation as in the previous experiment.

Materials:

Your choice of (dark, light - warm / cool + another colour) non-paint, opaque or transparent paint.

Two brushes (if using paint), white toned or coloured paper (a little larger).

Begin:

Copy same part of the still life from your MMM observation (object).

Use thin paint (large brush).

Only show what is necessary.

Then:

Use the dark and light colours to show still life forms and soft and hard edges for modelling.

Use thin paint before using thick paint and paint smaller parts later.

Paint unimportant areas before important parts.

Use soft and hard edges for modelling the form.

Boundaries between shapes should not always be too sharp or clear cut.

A soft irregular transition is required from time to time.

Develop your experiment but do NOT overwork it.

Gradually modify tones and colours – for example use warm and cool colour to show depth.

Suggest texture by dry-brush or sgraffito techniques which may require thicker paint.

Do not attempt too much detail - only paint what can be seen by a viewer.

Conclude:
Clean up.

UNIT 1: Experiment 4

Start with a different MMM still life observation.

Materials:

Your choice of (dark, light - warm / cool + another colour) non-paint, opaque or transparent paint.

Two brushes (if using paint), white toned or coloured paper (a little larger).

Begin:

Copy same part of the still life from your MMM observation (object).

Use thin paint (large brush) and only show what is necessary.

Then:

Use the dark and light colours to show still life form.

Use thin paint before using thick paint.

Paint unimportant areas before important parts.

Paint smaller parts later.

Use soft and hard edges for modelling the form.

Develop your experiment but do NOT overwork it.

Gradually modify tones and colours – for example use warm and cool colour to show depth.

Suggest texture by dry-brush or sgraffito techniques – may require thicker paint.

Do not attempt too much detail - only paint what can be seen by a viewer.

Conclude:

Clean up.

UNIT 1: Experiment 5

Start with a different MMM still life observation.

Materials:

Your choice of (dark, light - warm / cool + another colour) non-paint, opaque or transparent paint.

Two brushes (if using paint), white toned or coloured paper (a little larger).

Begin:

Copy same part of the still life from your MMM observation (object).

Include an extra component (dish, kennel, environment)

Use thin paint (large brush) and only show what is necessary.

Then:

Note the direction of the light.

Use the dark and light colours to show still life form.

At the same time establish the light source.

Paint unimportant areas before important parts.

Paint the background to establish brightness of the painting (light/dark).

Use thin paint before using thick paint.

Paint smaller parts later.

Use soft and hard edges for modelling the form.

Develop your experiment but do NOT overwork it.

Gradually modify tones and colours – for example use warm and cool colour to show depth.

Suggest texture by dry-brush or sgraffito techniques – may require thicker paint.

Do not attempt too much detail - only paint what can be seen by a viewer.
Conclude:
Clean up.

UNIT 1: Experiment 6
Start with a different MMM still life observation.
Materials:
Your choice of (dark, light - warm / cool + another colour) non-paint, opaque or transparent paint.
Two brushes (if using paint), white toned or coloured paper (a little larger).
Begin:
Copy same part of the still life from your MMM observation (object).
Include an extra component (dish, kennel, environment)
Use thin paint (large brush) and only show what is necessary.
Then:
Note the direction of the light.
Use dark and light colours to show still life form and at the same time establish the light source.
Paint unimportant areas before important parts.
Paint the background to establish brightness of the painting (light/dark).
Use thin paint before using thick paint and paint smaller parts later.
Use soft and hard edges for modelling the form.
Develop your experiment but do NOT overwork it.
Gradually modify tones and colours – for example use warm and cool colour to show depth.
Suggest texture by dry-brush or sgraffito techniques – may require thicker paint.
Do not attempt too much detail - only paint what can be seen by a viewer.

Conclude:
Clean up.

Further thoughts:
Use other observations of your own to explore other views.
Suggest still life shape by painting background first.
Paint a still life with as few brushstrokes as possible.

SECOND Experience Unit:

UNIT 2: Experiment 1
Start based on an MMM still life observation you have made.
Materials:
Your choice of (dark, light - warm / cool + another colour) non-paint, opaque or transparent paint.
Two brushes (if using paint), white toned or coloured paper (a little larger).
Begin:
Copy a different part of the still life from your MMM observation (object).
Include an extra component (dish, kennel, environment)
Paint the background to establish brightness of the painting (light/dark).
Use thin paint (large brush) and only show what is necessary.
Then:
Establish a single source for the light.
Use the dark and light colours to show still life form.
Use thin paint before using thick paint.
Paint unimportant areas before important parts.
Paint smaller parts later.
Use soft and hard edges for modelling the form.
Develop your experiment but do NOT overwork it.
Gradually modify tones and colours – for example use warm and cool colour to show depth.

Suggest texture by dry-brush or sgraffito techniques.

Under-paint area before laying on thicker paint.

Conclude:

Clean up.

UNIT 2: Experiment 2

Base start on a different MMM still life observation used in the previous experiment.

Materials:

Your choice of (dark, light - warm / cool + still life colour) non-paint, opaque or transparent paint.

Two brushes (if using paint), white toned or coloured paper (a little larger).

Begin:

Copy same part of the still life from your MMM observation (object).

Use thin paint (large brush) and only show what is necessary.

Include an extra component (dish, kennel, environment)

Paint the background to establish brightness of the painting (light/dark).

Then:

Establish a single source for the light and use the dark and light colours to show still life objects.

Use thin paint before using thick paint.

Paint unimportant areas before important parts and paint smaller parts later.

Use soft and hard edges for modelling the form.

Develop your experiment but do NOT overwork it.

Gradually modify tones and colours – for example use warm and cool colour to show depth.

Suggest texture by dry-brush or sgraffito techniques.

Under-paint area before laying on thicker paint.

Conclude:

Clean up.

UNIT 2: Experiment 3

Base start on a different MMM still life observation used in the previous experiment.

Materials:

Your choice of (dark, light - warm / cool + still life colour) non-paint, opaque or transparent paint.

Two brushes (if using paint), white toned or coloured paper (a little larger).

Begin:

Copy same part of the still life from your MMM observation (object).

Use thin paint (large brush) and only show what is necessary.

Include an extra component (dish, kennel, environment)

Paint the background to establish brightness of the painting (light/dark).

Then:

Establish direction of the light with the dark and light colours to show still life form.

Use thin paint before using thick paint.

Paint unimportant areas before important parts.

Work from most distant to closest areas and paint smaller parts later.

Use soft and hard edges for modelling the form.

Develop your experiment but do NOT overwork it.

Gradually modify tones and colours – for example use warm and cool colour to show depth.

Suggest texture by dry-brush or sgraffito techniques and under-paint beforehand.

Conclude:
Clean up.

UNIT 2: Experiment 4
Base start on a different MMM still life observation used in the previous experiment.
Materials:
Your choice of (dark, light - warm / cool + still life colour) non-paint, opaque or transparent paint.
Two brushes (if using paint), white toned or coloured paper (a little larger).
Begin:
Copy same part of the still life from your MMM observation (object).
Use thin paint (large brush) and only show what is necessary.
Include an extra component (dish, kennel, environment)
Paint the background to establish brightness of the painting (light/dark).
Then:
Establish direction of the light then use the dark and light colours to show still life form.
Use thin paint before using thick paint.
Paint unimportant areas before important parts.
Work from most distant to closest areas.
Paint smaller parts later.
Use soft and hard edges for modelling the form.
Develop your experiment but do NOT overwork it.
Gradually modify tones and colours – for example use warm and cool colour to show depth.

Suggest texture by dry-brush or sgraffito techniques and under-paint beforehand.

Conclude:

Clean up.

UNIT 2: Experiment 5

Base start on a different MMM still life observation used in the previous experiment.

Materials:

Your choice of (dark, light - warm / cool + still life colour) non-paint, opaque or transparent paint.

Two brushes (if using paint), white toned or coloured paper (a little larger).

Begin:

Copy same part of the still life from your MMM observation (object).

Use thin paint (large brush) and only show what is necessary.

Include an extra component (dish, kennel, environment)

Paint the background to establish brightness of the painting (light/dark).

Then:

Establish direction of the light then use the dark and light colours to show still life form.

Use thin paint before using thick paint.

Paint unimportant areas before important parts.

Work from most distant to closest areas.

Paint smaller parts later.

Use soft and hard edges for modelling the form.

Develop your experiment but do NOT overwork it.

Gradually modify tones and colours – using cool before warm to show depth.

Suggest texture by dry-brush or sgraffito techniques and under-paint beforehand.

Conclude:
Clean up.

UNIT 2: Experiment 6

Base start on a different MMM still life observation used in the previous experiment.

Materials:
Your choice of (dark, light - warm / cool + still life colour) non-paint, opaque or transparent paint.
Two brushes (if using paint), white toned or coloured paper (a little larger).

Begin:
Copy same part of the still life from your MMM observation (object).
Use thin paint (large brush) and only show what is necessary.
Include an extra component (dish, kennel, environment)
Paint the background to establish brightness of the painting (light/dark).

Then:
Establish direction of the light then use the dark and light colours to show still life form.
Use thin paint before using thick paint.
Paint unimportant areas before important parts.
Work from most distant to closest areas.
Paint smaller parts later.
Use soft and hard edges for modelling the form.
Develop your experiment but do NOT overwork it.
Gradually modify tones and colours – using cool before warm to show depth.

Suggest texture by dry-brush or sgraffito techniques and under-paint beforehand.

Conclude:

Clean up.

Further thoughts:

Paint still life silhouettes.

Paint background to suggest shape of still life.

Paint a still life with as few brushstrokes as possible.

Use a spotlight to experiment with different sources and directions of lighting.

THIRD Experience Unit:

UNIT 3: Experiment 1

Start based on two different MMM still life observations you have made.

Materials:

Your choice of (dark, light - warm / cool + still life colour) non-paint, opaque or transparent paint.

Two brushes (if using paint), white toned or coloured paper (a little larger).

Begin:

Copy the same part of each still life from your MMM observation (objects).

Use thin paint (large brush) and only show what is necessary.

Paint the background to establish brightness of the painting (light/dark).

Then:

Establish direction of the light then use the dark and light colours to show still life form.

Use thin paint before using thick paint.

Paint unimportant areas before important parts.

Use larger brush for larger areas and paint smaller parts later.

Work from most distant to closest areas.

Use soft and hard edges for modelling the form.

Decide the dominant colours.

Develop your experiment but do NOT overwork it.

Gradually modify tones and colours – using cool before warm to show depth.

Suggest texture by dry-brush or sgraffito techniques and under-paint beforehand.

Conclude:

Clean up.

UNIT 3: Experiment 2

Start based on two different MMM still life observations you have made.

Materials:

Your choice of (dark, light - warm / cool + still life colour) non-paint, opaque or transparent paint.

Two brushes (if using paint), white toned or coloured paper (a little larger).

Begin:

Copy the same part of each still life from your MMM observation (objects).

Establish direction of the light then use the dark and light colours to show still life form.

Use thin paint (large brush) and only show what is necessary.

Paint unimportant areas before important parts.

Paint the background to establish brightness of the painting (light/dark).

Use larger brush for larger areas and paint smaller parts later using thin paint before thick paint.

Decide the dominant colours and under-paint accordingly.

Suggest texture by dry-brush or sgraffito techniques and under-paint beforehand.

Then:

Work from most distant to closest areas.

Use soft and hard edges for modelling the form.

Boundary between shapes isn't always sharp or precise.

51

Develop your experiment but do NOT overwork it.

Gradually modify tones and colours – using cool before warm to show depth.

Conclude:

Clean up.

UNIT 3: Experiment 3

Start based on two different MMM still life observations you have made.

Materials:

Your choice of (dark, light - warm / cool + still life colour) non-paint, opaque or transparent paint.

Two brushes (if using paint), white toned or coloured paper (a little larger).

Begin:

Copy a different part of each still life from your MMM observation (objects).

Copy the same part for each still life noting light source.

Paint unimportant areas before important parts.

Use thin paint (large brush) and only show what is necessary with thin paint before thick paint.

Use larger brush for larger areas and paint smaller parts later.

Decide the dominant colours and under-paint accordingly.

Suggest texture by dry-brush or sgraffito techniques and under-paint beforehand.

Then:

Note direction of the light and keep it consistent through the experiment.

Paint the background to establish brightness of the painting (light/dark).

Paint dark and light areas to show still life form and work from most distant to closest areas.

Use soft and hard edges for modelling - the boundary between shapes isn't always sharp.

Develop your experiment but do NOT overwork it.

Gradually modify tones and colours – using cool before warm to show depth.

Conclude:

Clean up.

UNIT 3: Experiment 4

Start based on three different MMM still life observations you have made.

Materials:

Your choice of (dark, light - warm / cool + still life colour) non-paint, opaque or transparent paint.

Two brushes (if using paint), white toned or coloured paper (a little larger).

Begin:

Copy the same part of each still life observed previously from MMM observation (objects).

Blend the two MMM still life observation memories plan the light source to unify the two images.

Use thin paint (large brush) and only show what is necessary with thin paint before thick paint.

Use larger brush for larger areas and paint smaller parts later.

Decide the dominant colours and under-paint accordingly.

Suggest texture by dry-brush or sgraffito techniques and under-paint beforehand.

Then:

Note direction of the light and keep it consistent through the experiment.

Paint the background to establish brightness of the painting (light/dark).

Paint dark and light areas to show still life form and work from most distant to closest areas.

Use soft and hard edges for modelling - the boundary between shapes isn't always sharp.

Develop your experiment but do NOT overwork it.

Gradually modify tones and colours – using cool before warm to show depth.

Conclude:

Clean up.

UNIT 3: Experiment 5

Start based on another different MMM still life observation you have made.

Materials:

Your choice of (dark, light - warm / cool + still life colour) non-paint, opaque or transparent paint.

Two brushes (if using paint), white toned or coloured paper (a little larger).

Begin:

Copy two different parts of the still life from the previous MMM observation (objects).

Plan the light source and paint unimportant areas before important parts.

Use thin paint (large brush) and only show what is necessary.

Use larger brush for larger areas and paint smaller parts later.

Use thin paint before using thick paint.

Decide the dominant colours and under-paint accordingly.

Suggest texture by dry-brush or sgraffito techniques and under-paint beforehand.

Then:

Note direction of the light and keep it consistent through the experiment.

Paint the background to establish brightness of the painting (light/dark).

Paint dark and light areas to show the form of the still life.

Use soft and hard edges for modelling the form.

Work from most distant to closest areas.

Boundary between shapes isn't always sharp or precise.

Develop your experiment but do NOT overwork it.

Gradually modify tones and colours – using cool before warm to show depth.

Conclude:

Clean up.

UNIT 3: Experiment 6

Start based on a different MMM still life observation you have made.

Materials:

Your choice of (dark, light - warm / cool + still life colour) non-paint, opaque or transparent paint.

Two brushes (if using paint), white toned or coloured paper (a little larger).

Begin:

Copy two different parts of the still life from the MMM observation (objects).

Plan the light source then paint unimportant areas before important parts.

Use thin paint (large brush) and only show what is necessary before using thick paint.

Use larger brush for larger areas and paint smaller parts later.

Decide the dominant colours and under-paint accordingly.

Suggest texture by dry-brush or sgraffito techniques and under-paint beforehand.

Then:

Note direction of the light and keep it consistent through the experiment.

Paint the background to establish brightness of the painting (light/dark).

Paint dark and light areas to show still life form and work from most distant to closest areas.

Use soft and hard edges for modelling - the boundary between shapes isn't always sharp.

Develop your experiment but do NOT overwork it.

Gradually modify tones and colours – using cool before warm to show depth.

Conclude:

Clean up.

Further thoughts:

Paint background to suggest shape of still life.

Paint a still life with as few brushstrokes as possible.

Use a spotlight to experiment with different sources and directions of lighting.

Focus on soft and hard edges for modelling the form of a still life.

DEVELOPMENT: Extensions

In the Development extension activities:

Draw on what you have learnt.

You can link what you have learned to your own goals.

DEVELOPMENT: Extension 1

Start with an MMM observation.

Materials:

Use the SAME materials as used in a previous experiment from Unit One.

Use the SAME MMM image as used in a previous experiment Unit One.

Begin:

BUT repeat only one of the experiments.

DEVELOPMENT: Extension 2

Start based on an MMM observation you have made.

Materials:

Use the SAME materials as used in a previous experiment from Unit Two.

Use the SAME MMM image as used in a previous experiment Unit Two.

Begin:

BUT repeat only one of the experiments.

DEVELOPMENT: Extension 3

Start based memory of an MMM observation you have made.

Materials:

Use the SAME materials as used in a previous experiment from Unit Three.

Use the SAMEMMM image as used in a previous experiment Unit Three.

Begin:

BUT repeat only one of the experiments.

NOW START: OBSERVED STILL LIFE 2

FIRST Experience Unit:

UNIT 1: Experiment 1

Start with a MMM still life observation you have made.

Materials:

Your choice of (dark, light - warm / cool / still life colour) non-paint, opaque or transparent paint.

Two brushes (if using paint), white toned or coloured paper (a little larger).

Begin:

Copy two different parts of the still life from the MMM observation (objects).

Plan the light source.

Paint unimportant areas before important parts.

Decide the dominant colours plan under-painting.

Use thin paint (larger brush) before using thick paint.

Only show what is necessary.

Paint smaller parts later.

Suggest texture by dry-brush or sgraffito techniques and under-paint beforehand.

Then:

Keep direction of light consistent through the experiment.

Paint the background to establish brightness of the painting (light/dark).

Paint dark and light areas to show the form of the still life.

Boundary between shapes isn't always sharp or precise.

Use soft and hard edges for modelling the form.

Work from most distant to closest areas.

Develop your experiment but do NOT overwork it.

Gradually modify tones and colours – using cool before warm to show depth.

Conclude:

Clean up.

UNIT 1: Experiment 2

Start with a MMM still life observation you have made.

Materials:

Your choice of (dark, light - warm / cool / still life colour) non-paint, opaque or transparent paint.

Two brushes (if using paint), white toned or coloured paper (a little larger).

Begin:

Copy two different parts of the still life from the MMM observation (objects).

Plan the light source and paint unimportant areas before important parts.

Decide the dominant colours plan under-painting.

Use thin paint (larger brush) before using thick paint.

Only show what is necessary and paint smaller parts later.

Suggest texture by dry-brush or sgraffito techniques and under-paint beforehand.

Then:

Keep direction of light consistent through the experiment.

Paint the background to establish brightness of the painting (light/dark).

Paint dark and light areas to show the form of the still life.

Boundary between shapes isn't always sharp or precise.

Use soft and hard edges for modelling the form.

Work from most distant to closest areas.

Develop your experiment but do NOT overwork it.

Gradually modify tones and colours – using cool before warm to show depth.

Conclude:

Clean up.

UNIT 1: Experiment 3

Start with a MMM still life observation you have made.

Materials:

Your choice of (dark, light - warm / cool + still life colour) non-paint, opaque or transparent paint.

Two brushes (if using paint), white toned or coloured paper (a little larger).

Begin: .

Copy two different parts of the still life from the MMM observation (objects).

Plan the light source.

Paint unimportant areas before important parts with thin (larger brush) before thick paint.

Decide the dominant colours and plan the under-painting to only show what is necessary.

Start with larger areas and paint smaller parts later.

Suggest texture by dry-brush or sgraffito techniques and under-paint beforehand.

Then:

Keep direction of light consistent through the experiment.

Paint the background to establish brightness of the painting (light/dark).

Paint dark and light areas to show the form of the still life.

Boundary between shapes isn't always sharp or precise.

Use soft and hard edges for modelling the form.

Work from most distant to closest areas.

Develop your experiment but do NOT overwork it.

Gradually modify tones and colours – using cool before warm to show depth.

Conclude:

Clean up.

UNIT 1: Experiment 4

Start with a MMM still life observation you have made.

Materials:

Your choice of (dark, light - warm / cool + still life colour) non-paint, opaque or transparent paint.

Two brushes (if using paint), white toned or coloured paper (a little larger).

Begin:

Copy two different parts of the still life from the MMM observation (objects).

Plan the light source.

Paint unimportant areas before important parts with thin (larger brush) before thick paint.

Decide the dominant colours.

Plan the under-painting to only show what is necessary.

Start with larger areas and paint smaller parts later.

Suggest texture by dry-brush or sgraffito techniques and under-paint beforehand.

Then:

Keep direction of light consistent through the experiment.

Paint the background to establish brightness of the still life (light/dark).

Work from most distant to closest areas.

Paint dark and light areas to show the form of the still life.

Boundary between shapes isn't always sharp or precise.

Use soft and hard edges for modelling the form.

Develop your experiment but do NOT overwork it.

Gradually modify tones and colours – using cool before warm to show depth.

Conclude:

Clean up.

UNIT 1: Experiment 5

Start with a MMM still life observation you have made.

Materials:

Your choice of (dark, light - warm / cool + still life colour) non-paint, opaque or transparent paint.

Two brushes (if using paint), white toned or coloured paper (a little larger).

Begin:

Copy two different parts of the still life from the MMM observation (objects).

Plan the light source and keep direction of light consistent through the experiment.

Paint unimportant areas before important parts with thin (larger brush) before thick paint.

Start with larger areas and paint smaller parts later.

Decide the dominant colours and plan the under-painting to only show what is necessary.

Suggest texture by dry-brush or sgraffito techniques and under-paint beforehand.

Then:

Paint the background to establish brightness of the still life (light/dark).

Work from most distant to closest areas.

Paint dark and light areas to show the form of the still life.

Use soft and hard edges for modelling the form.

Develop your experiment but do NOT overwork it.

Gradually modify tones and colours – using cool before warm to show depth.

Conclude:

Clean up.

UNIT 1: Experiment 6

Start with a MMM still life observation you have made.

Materials:

Your choice of (dark, light - warm / cool + still life colour) non-paint, opaque or transparent paint.

Two brushes (if using paint), white toned or coloured paper (a little larger).

Begin:

Copy three different parts of the still life from the MMM observation (objects).

Plan the light source and keep direction of light consistent through the experiment.

Paint unimportant areas before important parts with thin (larger brush) before thick paint.

Start with larger areas and paint smaller parts later.

Decide the dominant colours.

Plan the under-painting to only show what is necessary.

Suggest texture by dry-brush or sgraffito techniques and under-paint beforehand.

Then:

Paint the background to establish brightness of the still life (light/dark).

Work from most distant to closest areas.

Paint dark and light areas to show the form of the still life.

Use soft and hard edges for modelling the form.

Develop your experiment but do NOT overwork it.

Gradually modify tones and colours – using cool before warm to show depth.

Conclude:

Clean up.

Further thoughts:

Use different combinations of parts of the still life from the MMM observation (objects).

Try another still life.

SECOND Experience Unit:

UNIT 2: Experiment 1

Start with a MMM still life observation you have made.

Materials:

Your choice of (dark, light - warm / cool + still life colour) non-paint, opaque or transparent paint.

Three brushes (if using paint), white toned or coloured paper (a little larger).

Begin:

Copy three parts of the still life from a MMM observation (objects) but not whole still life.

Plan the light source and keep direction of light consistent through the experiment.

Paint unimportant areas before important parts with thin (larger brush) before thick paint.

Start with larger areas and paint smaller parts later.

Decide the dominant colours and plan the under-painting to only show what is necessary.

Suggest texture by dry-brush or sgraffito techniques and under-paint beforehand.

Then:

Paint the background to establish brightness of the still life (light/dark).

Work from most distant to closest areas.

Paint dark and light areas to show the form of the still life.

Use soft and hard edges for modelling the form.

Develop your experiment but do NOT overwork it.

Gradually modify tones and colours – using cool before warm to show depth.

Conclude:

Clean up.

UNIT 2: Experiment 2

Start with a MMM still life observation you have made.

Materials:

Your choice of (dark, light - warm / cool + still life colour) non-paint, opaque or transparent paint.

Three brushes (if using paint), white toned or coloured paper (a little larger).

Begin:

Copy three parts of the still life from a MMM observation (objects) but not whole still life.

Plan the light source and keep direction of light consistent through the experiment.

Paint unimportant areas before important parts with thin (larger brush) before thick paint.

Start with larger areas and paint smaller parts later.

Decide the dominant colours and plan the under-painting to only show what is necessary.

Suggest texture by dry-brush or sgraffito techniques and under-paint beforehand.

Then:

Paint the background to establish brightness of the still life (light/dark).

Work from most distant to closest areas.

Paint dark and light areas to show the form of the still life.

Use soft and hard edges for modelling the form.

Develop your experiment but do NOT overwork it.

Gradually modify tones and colours – using cool before warm to show depth.

Conclude:

Clean up.

UNIT 2: Experiment 3

Start with a MMM still life observation you have made.

Materials:

Your choice of (dark, light - warm / cool + still life colour) non-paint, opaque or transparent paint.

Three brushes (if using paint), white toned or coloured paper (a little larger).

Begin:

Copy three parts of the still life from a MMM observation (objects) but not whole still life.

Plan the light source and keep direction of light consistent through the experiment.

Paint unimportant areas before important parts with thin (larger brush) before thick paint.

Start with larger areas and paint smaller parts later.

Decide the dominant colours and plan the under-painting to only show what is necessary.

Suggest texture by dry-brush or sgraffito techniques and under-paint beforehand.

Then:

Paint the background to establish brightness of the still life (light/dark).

Work from most distant to closest areas.

Paint dark and light areas to show the form of the still life.

Use soft and hard edges for modelling the form.

Develop your experiment but do NOT overwork it.

Gradually modify tones and colours – using cool before warm to show depth.

Conclude:

Clean up.

UNIT 2: Experiment 4

Start with a MMM still life observation you have made.

Materials:

Your choice of (dark, light - warm / cool + still life colour) non-paint, opaque or transparent paint.

Three brushes (if using paint), white toned or coloured paper (a little larger).

Begin:

Copy the still life from a MMM observation (whole still life).

Plan the light source and keep direction of light consistent through the experiment.

Paint unimportant areas before important parts with thin (larger brush) before thick paint.

Start with larger areas and paint smaller parts later.

Decide the dominant colours and plan the under-painting to only show what is necessary.

Suggest texture by dry-brush or sgraffito techniques and under-paint beforehand.

Then:

Paint the background to establish brightness of the still life (light/dark).

Work from most distant to closest areas.

Paint dark and light areas to show the form of the still life.

Use soft and hard edges for modelling the form.

Develop your experiment but do NOT overwork it.

Gradually modify tones and colours – using cool before warm to show depth.

Conclude:

Clean up.

UNIT 2: Experiment 5

Start with a MMM still life observation you have made.

Materials:

Your choice of (dark, light - warm / cool + still life colour) non-paint, opaque or transparent paint.

Three brushes (if using paint), white toned or coloured paper (a little larger).

Begin:

Copy the still life from the MMM observation.

Plan the light source and keep direction of light consistent through the experiment.

Paint unimportant areas before important parts with thin before thick paint.

Large brushes before small brushes.

Start with larger areas and paint smaller parts later.

Decide the dominant colours and plan the under-painting to only show what is necessary.

Suggest texture by dry-brush or sgraffito techniques and under-paint beforehand.

Then:

Paint the background to establish brightness of the still life (light/dark).

Work from most distant to closest areas.

Paint dark and light areas to show the form of the still life.

Use soft and hard edges for modelling the form.

Develop your experiment but do NOT overwork it.

Gradually modify tones and colours – using cool before warm to show depth.

Conclude:

Clean up.

UNIT 2: Experiment 6

Start with a MMM still life observation you have made.

Materials:

Your choice of (dark, light - warm / cool + still life colour) non-paint, opaque or transparent paint.

Three brushes (if using paint), white toned or coloured paper (a little larger).

Begin:

Copy the still life from the MMM observation.

Plan the light source and keep direction of light consistent through the experiment.

Paint unimportant areas before important parts with thin before thick paint.

Large brushes before small brushes.

Start with larger areas and paint smaller parts later.

Decide the dominant colours and plan the under-painting to only show what is necessary.

Suggest texture by dry-brush or sgraffito techniques and under-paint beforehand.

Then:

Paint the background to establish brightness of the still life (light/dark).

Work from most distant to closest areas.

Paint dark and light areas to show the form of the still life.

Use soft and hard edges for modelling the form.

Develop your experiment but do NOT overwork it.

Gradually modify tones and colours – using cool before warm to show depth.

Conclude:

Clean up.

Further thoughts:

Experiment with different viewpoints of the still life (above, front, side).

Try different still life arrangements from time to time.

They are a similar combination of different elements.

Look for characteristic arrangements for that still life.

Correct colour can come later.

THIRD Experience Unit:

UNIT 3: Experiment 1

Start with a MMM still life observation you have made.

Materials:

Your choice of (dark, light - warm / cool + still life colour) non-paint, opaque or transparent paint.

Three brushes (if using paint), white toned or coloured paper (a little larger).

Begin:

Copy the still life from the MMM observation.

Plan the light source and keep direction of light consistent through the experiment.

Paint unimportant areas before important parts with thin before thick paint.

Large brushes before small brushes.

Start with larger areas and paint smaller parts later.

Decide the dominant colours and plan the under-painting to only show what is necessary.

Suggest texture by dry-brush or sgraffito techniques and under-paint beforehand.

Then:

Paint the background to establish brightness of the still life (light/dark).

Work from most distant to closest areas.

Paint dark and light areas to show the form of the still life.

Use soft and hard edges for modelling the form.

Develop your experiment but do NOT overwork it.

Gradually modify tones and colours – using cool before warm to show depth.

Conclude:

Clean up.

UNIT 3: Experiment 2

Start with a different MMM still life observation you have made.

Materials:

Your choice of (dark, light - warm / cool + still life colour) non-paint, opaque or transparent paint.

Three brushes (if using paint), white toned or coloured paper (a little larger).

Begin:

Copy the still life from the MMM observation.

Plan the light source and keep direction of light consistent through the experiment.

Paint unimportant areas before important parts with thin before thick paint.

Large brushes before small brushes.

Start with larger areas and paint smaller parts later.

Decide the dominant colours and plan the under-painting to only show what is necessary.

Suggest texture by dry-brush or sgraffito techniques and under-paint beforehand.

Then:

Paint the background to establish brightness of the still life (light/dark).

Work from most distant to closest areas.

Paint dark and light areas to show the form of the still life.

Use soft and hard edges for modelling the form.

Develop your experiment but do NOT overwork it.

Gradually modify tones and colours – using cool before warm to show depth.

Conclude:

Clean up.

UNIT 3: Experiment 3

Start with another MMM still life observation you have made.

Materials:

Your choice of (dark, light - warm / cool + still life colour) non-paint, opaque or transparent paint.

Three brushes (if using paint), white toned or coloured paper (a little larger).

Begin:

Copy the still life from the MMM observation.

Plan the light source and keep direction of light consistent through the experiment.

Paint unimportant areas before important parts with thin before thick paint.

Large brushes before small brushes.

Start with larger areas and paint smaller parts later.

Decide the dominant colours and plan the under-painting to only show what is necessary.

Suggest texture by dry-brush or sgraffito techniques and under-paint beforehand.

Then:

Paint the background to establish brightness of the still life (light/dark).

Work from most distant to closest areas.

Paint dark and light areas to show the form of the still life.

Use soft and hard edges for modelling the form.

Develop your experiment but do NOT overwork it.

Gradually modify tones and colours – using cool before warm to show depth.

Conclude:

Clean up.

UNIT 3: Experiment 4

Start with two MMM still life observations you have made.

Materials:

Your choice of (dark, light - warm / cool + still life colour) non-paint, opaque or transparent paint.

Three brushes (if using paint), white toned or coloured paper (a little larger).

Begin:

In your experiment combine the still life arrangements from the MMM observations.

Plan the light source and keep direction of light consistent through the experiment.

Paint unimportant areas before important parts with thin before thick paint.

Large brushes before small brushes.

Start with larger areas and paint smaller parts later.

Decide the dominant colours and plan the under-painting to only show what is necessary.

Suggest texture by dry-brush or sgraffito techniques and under-paint beforehand.

Then:

Paint the background to establish brightness of the still life (light/dark).

Work from most distant to closest areas.

Paint dark and light areas to show the form of the still life.

Use soft and hard edges for modelling the form.

Develop your experiment but do NOT overwork it.

Gradually modify tones and colours – using cool before warm to show depth.

Conclude:

Clean up.

UNIT 3: Experiment 5

Start with two MMM still life observations you have made.

Materials:

Your choice of (dark, light - warm / cool + still life colour) non-paint, opaque or transparent paint.

Three brushes (if using paint), white toned or coloured paper (a little larger).

Begin:

In your experiment combine the still life arrangements from the MMM observations.

Plan the light source and keep direction of light consistent through the experiment.

Paint unimportant areas before important parts with thin before thick paint.

Large brushes before small brushes.

Start with larger areas and paint smaller parts later.

Decide the dominant colours and plan the under-painting to only show what is necessary.

Suggest texture by dry-brush or sgraffito techniques and under-paint beforehand.

Then:

Paint the background to establish brightness of the still life (light/dark).

Work from most distant to closest areas.

Paint dark and light areas to show the form of the still life.

Use soft and hard edges for modelling the form.

Develop your experiment but do NOT overwork it.

Gradually modify tones and colours – using cool before warm to show depth.

Conclude:

Clean up.

UNIT3: Experiment 6

Start with several MMM still life observations you have made.

Materials:

Your choice of (dark, light - warm / cool + still life colour) non-paint, opaque or transparent paint.

Three brushes (if using paint), white toned or coloured paper (a little larger).

Begin:

In your experiment combine the still life arrangements from the MMM observations as a group.

Plan the light source and keep direction of light consistent through the experiment.

Paint unimportant areas before important parts with thin before thick paint.

Large brushes before small brushes.

Start with larger areas and paint smaller parts later.

Decide the dominant colours and plan the under-painting to only show what is necessary.

Suggest texture by dry-brush or sgraffito techniques and under-paint beforehand.

Then:

Paint the background to establish brightness of the still life (light/dark).

Work from most distant to closest areas.

Paint dark and light areas to show the form of the still life.

Use soft and hard edges for modelling the form.

Develop your experiment but do NOT overwork it.

Gradually modify tones and colours – using cool before warm to show depth.

Conclude:

Clean up.

Further thoughts:
Experiment with different groups of the still life.
Also experiment with different viewpoints (top, side, rear, front,) of the still life.
Try different still life arrangements from time to time.
They are a similar combination of different elements.
Look for characteristic arrangements for that still life.
Correct colour can come later.

Make a study box.
Cut down a box so it is like a small room with a floor and two or even three sides.
Toy still life arrangements can be placed in the study box.
The floor and walls can be painted differently from time to time.

DEVELOPMENT: Extensions

In the Development extension activities:

Draw on what you have learnt.

You can link what you have learned to your own goals.

DEVELOPMENT: Extension 1

Start with an MMM observation.

Materials:

Use the SAME materials as used in a previous experiment from Unit One.

Use the SAME MMM image as used in a previous experiment Unit One.

Begin:

BUT repeat only one of the experiments.

DEVELOPMENT: Extension 2

Start based on an MMM observation you have made.

Materials:

Use the SAME materials as used in a previous experiment from Unit Two.

Use the SAME MMM image as used in a previous experiment Unit Two.

Begin:

BUT repeat only one of the experiments.

DEVELOPMENT: Extension 3

Start based memory of an MMM observation you have made.

Materials:

Use the SAME materials as used in a previous experiment from Unit Three.

Use the SAME MMM image as used in a previous experiment Unit Three.

Begin:

BUT repeat only one of the experiments.

CONGRATULATIONS.

You have taken the OBSERVATION pathway.
This continues from the previous pattern of experiments.
The focus is on observation as a basis for a continuing search for reality.
This could be the final step to being the artist you want to be.

But perhaps you want to try them all?
Then follow the sequence of MMM experiments as outlined there is a logical progression.

The third pathway is linked to your IMAGINATION.
This focus is more personal.
But again there is a foundation from the MMM experiments.

Your MMM experiments are like the athletes training program.
But the training never stops.
Like the Olympic athlete while you want to remain at the highest level you must keep training.
Your MMM experiments become a normal routine.

Make notes, do sketches and record what you can see.
This is material you can draw on when continuing your MMM experiments.
Make a habit of carrying a small sketchpad or even scraps of paper and a pen or pencil.

Perhaps start each day with a short period of experiments.
Then move to your main artistic tasks.

You will need to be able to construct YOUR OWN MMM experimental programs.
By now this should not be difficult.

IMAGINARY STILL LIFE.

Limited materials will encourage more thoughtful responses.
Creativity, an ability to do most with least, is developed.
In art as in science the task of combining many variables is highly skilled.
Repeat something rather than use too great a variety of materials.

The artist, during the act of creating a work is expressing something.
Expression is a unique personal action.

Three artists attempt to paint the same subject, exactly as seen.
They will finish with three different works.
The differences can be attributed to the various artists' expression.
Their works are symbols for this expression.

Expression is related to emotion.
Although the individual may not be conscious of what that emotion is.
The presence of emotion creates a tension (a feeling).
The tension isn't necessarily the emotion, but awareness of an emotional state.

Expression is bringing into perceptual form symbols for that awareness.
It is thus related to that the underlying emotional state.

The expressive act is not necessarily related to any particular audience.
There's a difference between intended arousing of emotion in an audience.
This is manipulative and a form of communication.

A similar arousal can be the result of expression.
Such expression denotes and belongs to an individual.
It is actually a characteristic of individuals.
It isn't communication although observers are often mistaken in this regard.

There's a difference between emotion and exhibiting it's symptoms.
The former is necessary for art activity and is a personal reaction to a stimulus.
Symptoms of emotion are what an observer sees.
They may manipulate the appropriate symbols without emotion at all (actor).

The relationship between an artist and the work is thus a personal one.
It's linked to an inner state of the artist prior to, and during, the creating.
That may ultimately be a work of art.

It doesn't really matter what you do at the start.
The most important thing is to actually do something.
Let's see what happens here when I do this?

Random starts do not necessarily have to be the case.
You can plan your starts, but take your time.
Don't rush enjoy the experience and see what you can find out.

Once you begin, you can alter or change what you have done.
It's better to do something and be wrong, than do nothing.
Mistakes can be corrected, and you learn what not to do at the same time.
Any experiment does not even have to be finished!

In the process you'll discover whatever you find out.
More importantly the discoveries are yours.
They're part of your experience rather than just part of following instructions.

Your knowledge grows from your own experiences.
This is what real learning is about.
Experience and confidence grows for the more you do the better you'll get!

You are the judge of quality, which is a variable that changes over time.
You have old works you thought were excellent at the time they were done.
What are they like now?

Continue with the subject matter you want to paint really well.
That way you are continuing down the correct path (for you).
Your focus is always on still life.
But now you are imagining your chosen painting focus.
This means you are NOT limited to things you can actually look at.

You can make notes, do sketches and record what you can see.
This is material you can draw on when continuing your MMM experiments.
Make a habit to carry a small sketchpad or scraps of paper and a pen or pencil.

Your observation helps you understand still life.
Over time you will develop the individual paining skills needed.
You will also know how to paint your subject your way.
That means you can take liberties in regard to what you see.

Eventually you can focus on another subject.
If it is related to your original theme you will learn much quicker.
Then from one kind of still life to another is an example.
Totally imaginary still life arrangements are an extension of this process.

You'll note the similarities and also the differences.
Follow this pattern for long enough, and you'll be able to paint anything!

People who do things well also do them faster than those who don't.
That applies to painting just as much as anything else.
It's one of the indicators of skill.

By now you should have noticed that repetition helps skill development.
Several small paintings are better for learning than one larger one (more time).
That's how you can apply what you have learnt.

Skill in art, sport or even medicine is basically the same phenomenon.

It's practiced behaviour in action.

Most artists don't do anywhere near enough paintings to develop any real skill.

Work on several experiments at the same time increases productivity.
For you reduce wasted time.
If you run into a dead-end with one painting move to another for a fresh start.
When the initial painting is returned to, there is a different attitude.
Otherwise set it aside again.

Working on a number of experiments at the same time saves materials.
A particular colour can be applied to the work for which it was intended.
BUT there are bound to be other works where that same colour is appropriate.
When you buy paint, buy in quantity, but only use as needed.

Avoid major works.
They take time (years), usually done slowly and are often large and complex.
You'll tend to labour over them as you seek to do your best.
You might occasionally do a slightly larger experiment.

Focus on learning what you can.
Action with materials = technique.
Practiced techniques = skill.
Habitual technique + skill = style.

NOW START: IMAGINARY STILL LIFE

FIRST Experience Unit:

UNIT 1: Experiment 1
Imagine a distorted MMM image to start.
Materials:
Choose (dark, light - warm / cool + dominant colour) non-paint, opaque or transparent paint.
Three brushes (if using paint), white toned or coloured paper (a little larger).
Preparation:
Distort the still life from the MMM image in your experiment.
Add another image (not still life) into the experiment.
Decide the dominant colour.
Consider the tonal arrangement.
Think about the spaces
Begin:
Large brushes before small brushes.
Start with larger areas and paint smaller parts later – basic construction.
Paint unimportant areas before important parts but only what is essential.
Thin before thick paint.
Then:
Paint the background to establish brightness of the still life (light/dark).
Under-paint with the dominant colour.
Paint dark and light areas to show the form of the still life.
Now:
Gradually modify tones and colours – using cool before warm to show depth.
Use tone to show depth (perspective) – light to dark lightest tone most distant.
Continue:
Use soft and hard edges for modelling the form.
Dry-brush or sgraffito techniques suggest texture and under-paint beforehand.

Develop your experiment but do NOT overwork it.

Conclude: Clean up.

UNIT 1: Experiment 2

Imagine a distorted MMM image to start.

Materials:

Choice of (dark, light - warm / cool + dominant colour) non-paint, opaque or transparent paint.

Three brushes (if using paint), white toned or coloured paper (a little larger).

Preparation:

Distort the still life from the MMM image in your experiment.

Add another image (not still life) into the experiment.

Decide the dominant colour.

Consider the tonal arrangement.

Think about the spaces

Begin:

Start with larger areas and paint smaller parts later – basic construction.

Paint unimportant areas before important parts.

But only what is essential.

Then:

Paint the background to establish brightness of the still life (light/dark).

Under-paint with the dominant colour.

Paint dark and light areas to show the form of the still life.

Thin before thick paint.

Cool colour before warm.

Now:

Gradually modify tones and colours – using cool before warm to show depth.

Use tone to show depth (perspective) – darkest tone most distant.

Continue:

Use soft and hard edges for modelling the form.

Suggest texture by dry-brush or sgraffito techniques and under-paint beforehand.

Develop your experiment but do NOT overwork it.

Conclude:

Clean up.

UNIT 1: Experiment 3

Imagine a distorted MMM image to start.

Materials:

Choice of (dark, light - warm / cool + dominant colour) non-paint, opaque or transparent paint.

Three brushes (if using paint), white toned or coloured paper (a little larger).

Preparation:

Distort the still life from the MMM image in your experiment.

Add another image (not still life) into the experiment.

Decide the dominant colour.

Consider the tonal arrangement.

Think about the spaces

Begin:

Start with larger areas and paint smaller parts later – basic construction.

Paint unimportant areas before important parts.

But only what is essential.

Then:

Paint the background to establish brightness of the still life (light/dark).

Under-paint with the dominant colour.

Paint dark and light areas to show the form of the still life.

Thin before thick paint.

Cool colour before warm.

Now:

Gradually modify tones and colours – using cool before warm to show depth.

Use tone to show depth (perspective) – darkest tone most distant.

Continue:

Use soft and hard edges for modelling the form.

Suggest texture by dry-brush or sgraffito techniques and under-paint beforehand.

Develop your experiment but do NOT overwork it.

Conclude:

Clean up.

UNIT 1: Experiment 4

Imagine a distorted MMM image to start.

Materials:

Choice of (dark, light - warm / cool + dominant colour) non-paint, opaque or transparent paint.

Three brushes (if using paint), white toned or coloured paper (a little larger).

Preparation:

Distort the still life from the MMM image in your experiment.

Add two other images (not still life) into the experiment.

Decide the dominant colour.

Consider the tonal arrangement.

Think about the spaces

Begin:

Start with larger areas and paint smaller parts later – basic construction.

Paint unimportant areas before important parts.

But only what is essential.

Then:

Paint the background to establish brightness of the still life (light/dark).

Under-paint with the dominant colour.

Paint dark and light areas to show the form of the still life.

Thin before thick paint.

Cool colour before warm.

Now:

Gradually modify tones and colours – using cool before warm to show depth.

Use tone to show depth (perspective) – darkest tone most distant.

Continue:

Use soft and hard edges for modelling the form.

Suggest texture by dry-brush or sgraffito techniques and under-paint beforehand.

Develop your experiment but do NOT overwork it.

Conclude:

Clean up.

UNIT 1: Experiment 5

Imagine a distorted MMM image to start.

Materials:

Choice of (dark, light - warm / cool + dominant colour) non-paint, opaque or transparent paint.

Three brushes (if using paint), white toned or coloured paper (a little larger).

Preparation:

Distort the still life from the MMM image in your experiment.

Add two other images (not still life) into the experiment.

Decide the dominant colour.

Consider the tonal arrangement.

Think about the spaces

Begin:

Start with larger areas and paint smaller parts later – basic construction.

Paint unimportant areas before important parts.

But only what is essential.

Then:

Paint the background to establish brightness of the still life (light/dark).

Under-paint with the dominant colour.

Paint dark and light areas to show the form of the still life.

Thin before thick paint.

Cool colour before warm.

Now:

Gradually modify tones and colours – using cool before warm to show depth.

Use tone to show depth (perspective) – darkest tone most distant.

Continue:

Use soft and hard edges for modelling the form.

Suggest texture by dry-brush or sgraffito techniques and under-paint beforehand.

Develop your experiment but do NOT overwork it.

Conclude:

Clean up.

UNIT 1: Experiment 6

Imagine a distorted MMM image to start.

Materials:

Choice of (dark, light - warm / cool + dominant colour) non-paint, opaque or transparent paint.

Three brushes (if using paint), white toned or coloured paper (a little larger).

Preparation:

Distort the still life from the MMM image in your experiment.

Add two other images (not still life) into the experiment.

Decide the dominant colour.

Consider the tonal arrangement.

Think about the spaces

Begin:

Start with larger areas and paint smaller parts later – basic construction.

Paint unimportant areas before important parts.

But only what is essential.

Then:

Focus experiment on colour.

Paint the background to establish brightness of the still life (light/dark).

Under-paint with the dominant colour.

Paint dark and light areas to show the form of the still life.

Thin before thick paint.

Cool colour before warm.

Now:

Gradually modify tones and colours – using cool before warm to show depth.

Use tone to show depth (perspective) – darkest tone most distant.

Continue:

Use soft and hard edges for modelling the form.

Suggest texture by dry-brush or sgraffito techniques and under-paint beforehand.

Develop your experiment but do NOT overwork it.

Conclude:

Clean up.

Further thoughts:

Experiment with the focus on different elements (colour, tone, shape, line, etc).

Also experiment with different principles (harmony, contrast, etc).

Also vary the viewpoint of your imaginary still life.

SECOND Experience Unit:

UNIT 2: Experiment 1

Imagine a semi-abstract MMM image to start.

Consider the visual element: Space

The factor that indicates emptiness or a break.

Space relates to the lack of obvious other element (particularly mass and line).

However space usually relates to being inside, outside, under or over.

Space may be open (incomplete) or closed (has a boundary).

Space also may be actual or implied.

It is sometimes termed environment.

Materials:

Choice of (dark, light - warm / cool + dominant colour) non-paint, opaque or transparent paint.

Three brushes (if using paint), white toned or coloured paper (a little larger).

Preparation:

Distort the still life from the MMM image in your experiment.

Add two or more other images (not still life) into the experiment.

Decide the dominant colour.

Consider the tonal arrangement.

Think about the spaces

Begin:

Start with larger areas and paint smaller parts later – basic construction.

Paint unimportant areas before important parts.

But only what is essential.

Then:

Focus experiment on colour.

Paint the background to establish brightness of the still life (light/dark).

Under-paint with the dominant colour.

Paint dark and light areas to show the form of the still life.

Thin before thick paint.

Cool colour before warm.

Now:

Gradually modify tones and colours – using cool before warm to show depth.

Use tone to show depth (perspective) – lightest tone most distant.

Continue:

Use soft and hard edges for modelling the form.

Suggest texture by dry-brush or sgraffito techniques and under-paint beforehand.

Develop your experiment but do NOT overwork it.

Conclude:

Clean up.

UNIT 2: Experiment 2

Imagine a semi-abstract MMM image to start.

Consider the visual element: Space

The factor that indicates emptiness or a break.

Space relates to the lack of obvious other element (particularly mass and line).

However space usually relates to being inside, outside, under or over.

Space may be open (incomplete) or closed (has a boundary).

Space also may be actual or implied.

Materials:

Choice of (dark, light - warm / cool + dominant colour) non-paint, opaque or transparent paint.

Three brushes (if using paint), white toned or coloured paper (a little larger).

Preparation:

Distort the still life from the MMM image in your experiment.

Add two or more other images (not still life) into the experiment.

Decide the dominant colour.

Consider the tonal arrangement.

Think about the spaces

Begin:

Start with larger areas and paint smaller parts later – basic construction.

Paint unimportant areas before important parts.

But only what is essential.

Then:

Focus experiment on colour.

Paint the background to establish brightness of the still life (light/dark).

Under-paint with the dominant colour.

Paint dark and light areas to show the form of the still life.

Thin before thick paint.

Cool colour before warm.

Now:

Gradually modify tones and colours – using cool before warm to show depth.

Use tone to show depth (perspective) – darkest tone most distant.

Continue:

Use soft and hard edges for modelling the form.

Suggest texture by dry-brush or sgraffito techniques and under-paint beforehand.

Develop your experiment but do NOT overwork it.

Conclude:

Clean up.

UNIT 2: Experiment 3

Imagine a semi-abstract MMM image to start.

Consider the visual element: Space

The factor that indicates emptiness or a break.

However space usually relates to being inside, outside, under or over.

Space may be open (incomplete) or closed (has a boundary).

Space also may be actual or implied.

Materials:

Choice of (dark, light - warm / cool + dominant colour) non-paint, opaque or transparent paint.

Three brushes (if using paint), white toned or coloured paper (a little larger).

Preparation:

Distort the still life from the MMM image in your experiment.

Add two or more other distorted images (not still life) into the experiment.

Decide the dominant colour.

Consider the tonal arrangement.

Think about the spaces

Begin:

Start with larger areas and paint smaller parts later – basic construction.

Paint unimportant areas before important parts.

But only what is essential.

Then:

Focus experiment on colour.

Paint the background to establish brightness of the still life (light/dark).

Under-paint with the dominant colour.

Paint dark and light areas to show the form of the still life.

Thin before thick paint.

Cool colour before warm.

Now:

Gradually modify tones and colours – using cool before warm to show depth.

Use tone to show depth (perspective) – lightest and darkest tone closest with grey most distant.

Continue:

Use soft and hard edges for modelling the form.

Suggest texture by dry-brush or sgraffito techniques and under-paint beforehand.

Develop your experiment but do NOT overwork it.

Conclude:

Clean up.

UNIT 2: Experiment 4

Imagine a semi-abstract MMM image to start.

Consider the visual element: Space

Space usually relates to being inside, outside, under or over.

Space may be open (incomplete) or closed (has a boundary).

Space also may be actual or implied.

Materials:

Choice of (dark, light - warm / cool + dominant colour) non-paint, opaque or transparent paint.

Three brushes (if using paint), white toned or coloured paper (a little larger).

Preparation:

Distort the still life from the MMM image in your experiment.

Add two or more other distorted images (not still life) into the experiment.

Decide the dominant colour.

Consider the tonal arrangement.

Think about the spaces

Begin:

Start with larger areas and paint smaller parts later – basic construction.

Paint unimportant areas before important parts.

But only what is essential.

Then:

Focus experiment on colour.

Paint the background to establish brightness of the still life (light/dark).

Under-paint with the dominant colour.

Paint dark and light areas to show the form of the still life.

Thin before thick paint.

Cool colour before warm.

Now:

Gradually modify tones and colours – using cool before warm to show depth.

Tone to show depth (perspective) – lightest and darkest closest - grey distant.

Continue:

Use soft and hard edges for modelling the form.

Suggest texture by dry-brush or sgraffito - and under-paint beforehand.

Develop your experiment but do NOT overwork it.

Conclude: Clean up.

UNIT 2: Experiment 5

Imagine a semi-abstract MMM image to start.

Consider the visual element: Space

Space may be open (incomplete) or closed (has a boundary).

Space also may be actual or implied.

Materials:

Choice of (dark, light - warm / cool + dominant colour) non-paint, opaque or transparent paint.

Three brushes (if using paint), white toned or coloured paper (a little larger).

Preparation:

Distort the still life from the MMM image in your experiment.

Add 2+ overlapping and distorted images (not still life) to the experiment.

Decide the dominant colour.

Consider the tonal arrangement.

Think about the spaces

Begin:

Start with larger areas and paint smaller parts later – basic construction.

Paint unimportant areas before important parts.

But only what is essential.

Then:

Focus experiment on colour.

Paint the background to establish brightness of the still life (light/dark).

Under-paint with the dominant colour.

Paint dark and light areas to show the form of the still life.

Thin before thick paint.

Cool colour before warm.

Now:

Gradually modify tones and colours – using cool before warm to show depth.

Tone to show depth (perspective) – lightest and darkest closest, grey distant.

Continue:

Use soft and hard edges for modelling the form.

Suggest texture by dry-brush or sgraffito techniques and under-paint beforehand.

Develop your experiment but do NOT overwork it.

Conclude: Clean up.

UNIT 2: Experiment 6

Imagine a semi-abstract MMM image to start.

Consider the visual element: Space

Space may be open (incomplete) or closed (has a boundary).

Materials:

Choice of (dark, light - warm / cool + dominant colour) non-paint, opaque or transparent paint.

Three brushes (if using paint), white toned or coloured paper (a little larger).

Preparation:

Distort the still life from the MMM image in your experiment.

Add 2+ overlapping and distorted images (not still life) into the experiment.

Decide the dominant colour.

Consider the tonal arrangement.

Think about the spaces

Begin:

Start with larger areas and paint smaller parts later – basic construction.

Paint unimportant areas before important parts.

But only what is essential.

Then:

Focus experiment on colour.

Paint the background to establish brightness of the still life (light/dark).

Under-paint with the dominant colour.

Paint dark and light areas to show the form of the still life.

Thin before thick paint.

Cool colour before warm.

Now:

Gradually modify tones and colours – using cool before warm to show depth.

Use tone to show depth (perspective) – lightest darkest closest, grey distant.

Continue:

Refocus on the dominant colour and modify local colour accordingly.

Use soft and hard edges for modelling the form.

Suggest texture by dry-brush or sgraffito techniques and under-paint beforehand.

Develop your experiment but do NOT overwork it.

Conclude: Clean up.

Further thoughts:

Also experiment with different principles (harmony, contrast, etc).

Also vary the viewpoint of your imaginary still life.

Still life arrangements have their own colour (local colour).

This could be any colour if you paint consistently.

THIRD Experience Unit:

UNIT 3: Experiment 1

Imagine two semi-abstracted MMM images to start.

Consider the visual element: Direction

The factor that indicates aim or course of movement.

The movement may be real or suggested.

Direction relates to a plane or axis, which may be horizontal, vertical or oblique.

There is a start and an end and can be seen in a serial order or sequence.

There is a link with rhythm and balance.

Materials:

Choice non-paint, opaque or transparent paint (dark, light, dominant, complementary) colours.

Three brushes (if using paint), white toned or coloured paper (a little larger).

Preparation:

Distort the still life arrangements from the MMM images in your experiment.

Add two or more overlapping and distorted images (not still life) into the experiment.

Decide the dominant colour.

Consider the tonal arrangement.

Think about the spaces

Begin:

Start with larger areas and paint smaller parts later – basic construction.

Paint unimportant areas before important parts.

But only what is essential.

Then:

Under-paint with the dominant colour.

Thin before thick paint.

Cool colour before warm.

Now:

Gradually modify tones and colours.

Use tone to show depth (perspective) – lightest and darkest tone closest with grey most distant.

Continue:

Refocus on the dominant colour and modify local colour accordingly.

Use the complementary (opposite) colours in short brushstrokes next to one another.

Use soft and hard edges for modelling.

Suggest texture by dry-brush or sgraffito techniques and under-paint beforehand.

Develop your experiment but do NOT overwork it.

Conclude:

Clean up.

UNIT 3: Experiment 2

Imagine two semi-abstracted MMM images to start.

Consider the visual element: Direction

The factor that indicates aim or course of movement.

The movement may be real or suggested.

Direction relates to a plane or axis, which may be horizontal, vertical or oblique.

There is a start and an end and can be seen in a serial order or sequence.

Materials:

Choice non-paint, opaque or transparent paint (dark, light, dominant, complementary) colours.

Three brushes (if using paint), white toned or coloured paper (a little larger).

Preparation:

Distort the still life arrangements from the MMM images in your experiment.

Add two or more overlapping and distorted images (not still life) into the experiment.

Decide the dominant colour.

Consider the tonal arrangement.

Think about the spaces

Begin:

Start with larger areas and paint smaller parts later – basic construction.

Paint unimportant areas before important parts.

But only what is essential.

Then:

Under-paint with the dominant colour.

Thin before thick paint.

Cool colour before warm.

Now:

Gradually modify tones and colours.

Use tone to show depth (perspective) – lightest and darkest tone closest with grey most distant.

Continue:

Refocus on the dominant colour and modify local colour accordingly.

Scumble the complementary (opposite) colours in light brushstrokes one on top of the other.

Use soft and hard edges for modelling.

Suggest texture by dry-brush or sgraffito techniques and under-paint beforehand.

Develop your experiment but do NOT overwork it.

Conclude:

Clean up.

UNIT 3: Experiment 3

Imagine two semi-abstracted MMM images to start.

Consider the visual element: Direction

The factor that indicates aim or course of movement.

Direction relates to a plane or axis, which may be horizontal, vertical or oblique.

There is a start and an end and can be seen in a serial order or sequence.

Materials:

Choice non-paint, opaque or transparent paint (dark, light, dominant, complementary) colours.

Three brushes (if using paint), white toned or coloured paper (a little larger).

Preparation:

Distort the still life arrangements from the MMM images in your experiment.

Add two or more overlapping and distorted images (not still life) into the experiment.

Decide the dominant colour.

Consider the tonal arrangement.

Think about the spaces

Begin:

Concentrate on the basic construction of your experiment.

Paint unimportant areas before important parts.

But only what is essential.

Then:

Under-paint with the dominant colour.

Thin before thick paint.

Cool colour before warm.

Now:

Gradually modify tones and colours.

Use tone to show depth (perspective) – lightest and darkest tone closest with grey most distant.

Continue:

Refocus on the dominant colour and modify local colour accordingly.

Use a pointillist technique - complementary (opposite) colours in small dots next to each other.

Use soft and hard edges for modelling.

Suggest texture by dry-brush or sgraffito techniques and under-paint beforehand.

Develop your experiment but do NOT overwork it.

Conclude:

Clean up.

UNIT 3: Experiment 4

Imagine two semi-abstracted MMM images to start.

Consider the visual element: Direction

The factor that indicates aim or course of movement.

Direction relates to a plane or axis, which may be horizontal, vertical or oblique.

Materials:

Choice dark, light, dominant, complementary colours (two harmonious one complementary).

Three brushes (if using paint), white toned or coloured paper (a little larger).

Preparation:

Distort the still life arrangements from the MMM images in your experiment.

Add two or more overlapping and distorted images (not still life) into the experiment.

Imagine some reflections of the semi-abstract still life images.

Decide the colour scheme (two harmonious one complementary).

Consider the tonal arrangement.

Think about the spaces

Begin:

Concentrate on the basic construction of your experiment.

Paint unimportant areas before important parts.

But only what is essential.

Then:

Under-paint with the dominant colour.

Thin before thick paint.

Cool colour before warm.

Now:

Gradually modify tones and colours.

Use tone to show depth (perspective) – lightest and darkest tone closest with grey most distant.

Reflections are upside down images.

If the surface is disturbed (water) reflections are darker.

A shiny or glossy surface takes some of the reflected local colour.

Continue:

Refocus on the dominant colour and modify local colour accordingly.

Use a pointillist technique - complementary (opposite) colours in small dots next to each other.

Use soft and hard edges for modelling.

Suggest texture by dry-brush or sgraffito techniques and under-paint beforehand.

Develop your experiment but do NOT overwork it.

Conclude:

Clean up.

UNIT 3: Experiment 5

Imagine two semi-abstracted MMM images to start.

Consider the visual element: Direction

The factor that indicates aim or course of movement.

Materials:

Choice dark, light, dominant, complementary colours (two harmonious one complementary).

The colours should be different from those used in the last experiment.

Three brushes (if using paint), white toned or coloured paper (a little larger).

Preparation:

Distort the still life arrangements from the MMM images in your experiment.

Add two or more overlapping and distorted images (not still life) into the experiment.

Imagine some reflections of the semi-abstract still life images.

Decide the colour scheme (two harmonious one complementary) but different from previously.

Consider the tonal arrangement.

Think about the spaces

Begin:

Concentrate on the basic construction of your experiment.

Paint unimportant areas before important parts.

But only what is essential.

Then:

Under-paint with the dominant colour.

Thin before thick paint.

Cool colour before warm.

Now:

Gradually modify tones and colours.

Use tone to show depth (perspective) – lightest and darkest tone closest with grey most distant.

Reflections are upside down images.

If the surface is disturbed (water) reflections are darker.

A shiny or glossy surface takes some of the reflected local colour.

Continue:

Refocus on the dominant colour and modify local colour accordingly.

Use a pointillist technique - complementary (opposite) colours in small dots next to each other.

Use soft and hard edges for modelling.

Suggest texture by dry-brush or sgraffito techniques and under-paint beforehand.

Develop your experiment but do NOT overwork it.

Conclude:

Clean up.

UNIT 3: Experiment 6

Imagine two semi-abstracted MMM images to start.

Consider the visual element: Direction

The factor that indicates aim or course of movement.

Materials:

Choice dark, light, dominant, complementary colours (two harmonious one complementary).

The colours should be different from those used in the last experiment.

Three brushes (if using paint), white toned or coloured paper (a little larger).

Preparation:

Distort the still life arrangements from the MMM images in your experiment.

Add two or more overlapping and distorted images (not still life) into the experiment.

Imagine some reflections of the semi-abstract still life images.

Decide the colour scheme (two harmonious one complementary) but different from previously.

Consider the tonal arrangement.

Think about the spaces

Begin:

Concentrate on the basic construction of your experiment.

Paint unimportant areas before important parts.

But only what is essential.

Then:

Under-paint with the dominant colour.

Thin before thick paint.

Cool colour before warm.

Now:

Gradually modify tones and colours.

Use tone to show depth (perspective) – lightest and darkest tone closest with grey most distant.

Reflections are upside down images.

If the surface is disturbed (water) reflections are darker.

A shiny or glossy surface takes some of the reflected local colour.

Continue:

Refocus on the dominant colour and modify local colour accordingly.

Use a pointillist technique - complementary (opposite) colours in small dots next to each other.

Use soft and hard edges for modelling.

Suggest texture by dry-brush or sgraffito techniques and under-paint beforehand.

Develop your experiment but do NOT overwork it.

Conclude:

Clean up.

Further thoughts:

Also continue to experiment so that the still life is totally abstract.

In other words it is just a shape within the experiment.

Continue to vary the viewpoint of your imaginary still life.

DEVELOPMENT: Extensions

In the Development extension activities:

Draw on what you have learnt.

You can link what you have learned to your own goals.

DEVELOPMENT: Extension 1

Imagine a distorted MMM image to start.

Materials:

Use the SAME materials as used in a previous experiment from Unit One.

Use the SAME MMM image as used in a previous experiment Unit One.

Begin:

BUT repeat only one of the experiments.

DEVELOPMENT: Extension 2

Imagine a semi-abstract MMM image to start.

Materials:

Use the SAME materials as used in a previous experiment from Unit Two.

Use the SAME MMM image as used in a previous experiment Unit Two.

Begin:

BUT repeat only one of the experiments.

DEVELOPMENT: Extension 3

Imagine an abstract MMM image to start.

Materials:
Use the SAME materials as used in a previous experiment from Unit Three.
Use the SAME MMM image as used in a previous experiment Unit Three.
Begin:
BUT repeat only one of the experiments.

CONGRATULATIONS.

You have taken the IMAGINATION pathway.
This continues from the previous pattern of experiments.
The focus is your imagination for a continuing search for personal reality.

This is the final step to being the artist you want to be.

Your MMM experiments are like the athletes training program.
Like an Olympic athlete to remain at the highest level you keep training.
Your MMM experiments become a normal routine.

Make notes, do sketches and record what you can see.
This is material you can draw on when continuing your MMM experiments.
Make a habit to carry a small sketchpad or scraps of paper and a pen or pencil.

Start each day with a short period of experiments.
Then move to your main artistic tasks.

You'll need to construct YOUR OWN MMM experimental programs.
By now this should not be difficult.

Planning major works could follow from that.
But do them as extensions of your MMM experiments.
A slightly larger experiment can develop into a major work.

Then much of the planning and preparatory work has been done.

WHERE NEXT?

You can buy an e-book:
Which is always the latest version.
OR
A printed book which is current at the time of purchase.
But will NOT be updated in the future.

There are other books that link with this book.
BUT they have a different focus.
You can specialize by completing ONE of the books.
But you can also complete as many of these books as you wish.
That could even be at different times.

Animals
http://www.amazon.com/dp/B08CP92NMW

Buildings
http://www.amazon.com/dp/B08CPJJTJS

Figures
http://www.amazon.com/dp/B08CPDL76B

Flowers
http://www.amazon.com/dp/B08CPLDRVT

Landscapes
http://www.amazon.com/dp/B08CPBJY1G

Portraits
http://www.amazon.com/dp/B08CPLDRW3

An Art Program is a background this book.
http://www.amazon.com/dp/1731347324
An Art Program book.
http://www.amazon.com/dp/B09GQSNY86

NOT NOW:

Perhaps one of these books could interest you then?

Write about your own memories?
http://www.amazon.com/dp/B087DWKPTP

A simple way to start developing creativity.
If you are a parent, teacher or who meet a group regularly?
http://www.amazon.com/dp/B088T1KFQZ

Starting an art career is NOW is harder than it ever was.
To help someone start – they download this link to their computer or ipad.
http://www.amazon.com/dp/B088T7VJ76

More of my memories
http://www.amazon.com/dp/B088Y4RPL9

SEND TO:

Know anyone interested in chocolate recipes?
Send them a link then.
http://www.amazon.com/dp/B088Y4RPL9

Know anyone interested in this book?
http://www.amazon.com/dp/B08CPLLXRB